for William Howard

24 Preludes and Fugues

HOWARD SKEMPTON

1

24 Preludes and Fugues were composed for William Howard who gave the first performance on 27 May 2019 at the Hay Festival, followed by the London premiere on 12 February 2020 at Kings Place. A recording of this work is available on the album *Howard Skempton: Piano Works*, released by Orchid Classics in 2020.

Duration: 22 mins

Printed in Great Britain

OXFORD UNIVERSITY PRESS, MUSIC DEPARTMENT, GREAT CLARENDON STREET, OXFORD OX2 6DP

Moderato

Larghetto

4

Allegretto

Andante

Moderato

Adagio

6

8

9

Moderato

Adagio

10

Allegro

Moderato

11

Andante

Adagio

12

Allegro

Largo

13

Andante

14

15

16

17

Adagio

18

Moderato

Andante

19

20

Adagio

21

Moderato

Andante

22

Adagio

23

Adagio

24

Allegro

Largo

Music originated by Julian Elloway
Printed in England by Halstan & Co. Ltd, Amersham, Bucks.